Letts

KS1

Success

Revision Guide

Paul Broadbent

Maths

Contents

Numbers

Calculations

Measures and shapes

Handling data

Test practice

Answers and glossary

Counting patterns

Counting objects

Counting is a really important part of maths – and **grouping is a quick way of counting objects**.

Count this set of shells.

Make sure you do not miss any out.

Did you count 20 shells?

Now **count them in twos: 2, 4, 6, 8...**

This can be a lot quicker.

You might even be able to **count in groups of five: 5, 10, 15, 20...**

Counting to 100

You need to know the numbers to 100. Use this 0–99 square to help you learn the positions of all the numbers. Remember that 34 is 30 + 4 and 67 is 60 + 7. So to find 67 go down to 60 and then across to 67.

0	1	2	3	4	5	6	7	8	9
10	11	12	13	14	15	16	17	18	19
20	21	22	23	24	25	26	27	28	29
30	31	32	33	34	35	36	37	38	39
40	41	42	43	44	45	46	47	48	49
50	51	52	53	54	55	56	57	58	59
60	61	62	63	64	65	66	67	68	69
70	71	72	73	74	75	76	77	78	79
80	81	82	83	84	85	86	87	88	89
90	91	92	93	94	95	96	97	98	99

I sometimes count sheep to help me get to sleep.

I find all that baaaaing keeps me awake...

Sequences

A **sequence** is a list of numbers with a pattern. They are often numbers written in order.

| 7 | 8 | 9 | 10 | 11 | | 43 | 42 | 41 | 40 |

If you are asked to write missing numbers from a sequence, look carefully at the numbers you are given. Try to work out the numbers next to these first and then fill out the others.

29 follows 28, then the next number is 30.
Which number follows 31?

| 27 | 28 | | 30 | |

Number patterns

You can count patterns in many **different steps**.

Look at these jumps in 2s, 5s and 10s:

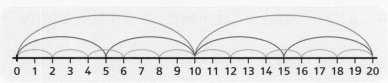

0 1 2 3 4 5 6 7 8 9 10 11 12 13 14 15 16 17 18 19 20

Top Tip

*To help you work out the missing number in a sequence, draw 'jumps' between each number and write the **difference** between them over each 'jump'.*

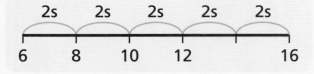

2s   2s   2s   2s   2s

6   8   10   12   16

Have a go...

Copy out the 0–99 square on page 4.
Play the following game with a friend:
• *Place small buttons to cover different numbers on the 100-square.*
• *Try to work out what the hidden numbers are.*

Key words

sequence   difference

Quick Test

Work out the missing numbers in these sequences:

1 28, 29, 30, ☐ , ☐ , 33

2 17, 19, 21, ☐ , 25, ☐

3 5, 10, ☐ , 20, ☐

4 90, 80, ☐ , 60, ☐

5 16, 14, 12, ☐ , ☐ , 6

Numbers

Teen numbers

It is easy to get in a muddle with the numbers between 10 and 20. You say them in a different way to the other numbers, so read these and make sure you know how to say each one:

11 eleven	14 fourteen	17 seventeen
12 twelve	15 fifteen	18 eighteen
13 thirteen	16 sixteen	19 nineteen

2-digit numbers

All our numbers are made from ten **digits**:

| 0 | 1 | 2 | 3 | 4 | 5 | 6 | 7 | 8 | 9 |

The position of these digits in a number makes each number different.

53 Fifty-three
This is 5 'tens'
and 3 'ones'.

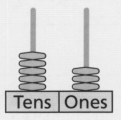

Tens | Ones

72 Seventy-two
This is 7 'tens'
and 2 'ones'.

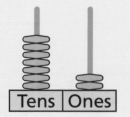

Tens | Ones

When you read a 2-digit number, it helps to break it up into tens and ones.

Top Tip

Our Gran acts like a teenager.

Yes - she's 71 but acts like she's 17!

More or less

Making a number **10 more or 10 less** is easy if you understand how numbers work.

For all these, **just the 'tens' change**.

10 more than 49 is 59

10 less than 84 is 74

10 more than 236 is 246

10 less than 462 is 452

3-digit numbers

Look at these numbers and how they are made:

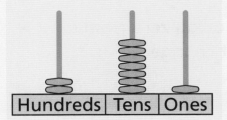

271 two hundred and seventy-one.

649 six hundred and forty-nine.

The position of a digit in a number is really important. 125 and 512 use the same digits, but they are very different numbers. Always check where you put each digit when you are writing out a number.

Have a go...

Go on a number hunt. Look around the house and in newspapers and write down ten numbers you can find. What is the BIGGEST number you can find?

Key words

digits

Quick Test

1. Which number comes after fourteen? Is it 51, 15 or 41?

2. What number is this?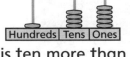

3. Which number is ten more than 263?

4. Which number is ten less than 487?

5. What is the largest number you can make with the digits 4, 7 and 6?

Special numbers

Zero the hero

0 is a special number with many names: zero, nothing, nought and nil.

Zero is used in different ways:

This number line starts with 0:

0 1 2 3 4 5 6

This poor leopard has lost all his spots.
He has 0 spots.

0s can mean big numbers too!
10, 20, 30, 40, 50... all end in 0 – and they are
big numbers.

> If you have to add zero to a number or take away zero from a
> number, remember that **the number does not change**.
>
> $$4 + 0 = 4 \qquad\qquad 6 - 0 = 6$$

Odd and even numbers

These are the odd and even numbers to 20.

Remember: **odd numbers always
end in 1, 3, 5, 7 or 9, and even
numbers always end in 0, 2, 4, 6 or 8.**

Even numbers can be divided by 2 and
odd numbers cannot be divided by 2.

Odd numbers			Even numbers		
1	3	5	2	4	6
7	9	11	8	10	12
13	15	17	14	16	18
	19			20	

I know
1 is an odd number,
because I can't put
this sock into a
pair.

Yes,
you're right -
that's is an odd
sock!

8

Multiples

It is useful to be able to recognise multiples of 2, 5 and 10.

Look at this 100-square to see what is special about these numbers.

Multiples of

2: end in 0, 2, 4, 6, 8.

5: end in 0 or 5.

10: end in 0.

Do you notice something about the multiples of 10 on the 100-square? They are also multiples of both 2 and 5.

1	2	3	4	5	6	7	8	9	10
11	12	13	14	15	16	17	18	19	20
21	22	23	24	25	26	27	28	29	30
31	32	33	34	35	36	37	38	39	40
41	42	43	44	45	46	47	48	49	50
51	52	53	54	55	56	57	58	59	60
61	62	63	64	65	66	67	68	69	70
71	72	73	74	75	76	77	78	79	80
81	82	83	84	85	86	87	88	89	90
91	92	93	94	95	96	97	98	99	100

Top Tip *Remember that even numbers are all multiples of 2.*

A dozen

Did you know...? A **dozen** is a special number – it means 12. People also talk about half-a-dozen – which is 6.

Have a go...

Write down:
- *3 odd numbers greater than 50*
- *3 multiples of 2*
- *3 multiples of 5*
- *3 multiples of 10.*
Make each number different.

Key words

zero	multiples
odd numbers	dozen
even numbers	

Quick Test

1. Is 27 an even or odd number?

2. If I had a dozen cream cakes and I ate 12 of them, how many would I have left?

3. Is 70 a multiple of 10?

4. Which number between 15 and 25 is a multiple of both 2 and 5?

5. What is the next multiple of 10 after 100?

Comparing and ordering

First things first

You may have seen numbers with 'st', 'th', 'rd' or 'nd' written after them. These strange endings show the **order or position of things**. Look at these and try to remember each one:

1st	3rd	5th	7th	9th

2nd	4th	6th	8th	10th

Comparing numbers

When you need to compare two numbers, you must look carefully at the **digits**. You might be asked to find the biggest or smallest.

For example, which is bigger: 36 or 63?

36 is the same as 30 + 6   63 is the same as 60 + 3   ➡   63 is bigger than 36

< and >

These are really useful symbols... but don't confuse them.

< means **is less than**. For example, 35 < 45   35 is less than 45.

> means **is greater than**. For example, 28 > 19   28 is greater than 19.

Halfway numbers

You might be asked to find a number halfway between two others. For example, what number is halfway between 9 and 13?

This is quite tricky to do in your head – so a good way of working it out is to **draw a number line**.

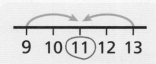

9 10 (11) 12 13

Ordering numbers

When you put numbers in order of size, order the 'tens' to start with, then order the 'ones'.

For example, put these numbers in order, starting with the smallest.

47, 36, 18, 29, 42

Use these two simple steps:

1st step: Just look at the 'tens' and write them in order:
18, 29, 36, 47, 42

2nd step: If any of the 'tens' are the same, put the 'ones' in order:
18, 29, 36, 42, 47

Number tracks

100-squares, number lines and number tracks are very useful for helping to learn the order of numbers.

Top Tip *If you find it difficult to put numbers in order, look carefully at a number track or 100-square, put it away and then try to picture where the numbers are on the track or square.*

Have a go...

Make a set of digit cards 1 to 9. Choose any three cards.

Write down all the different numbers you can make. For example, with 3, 6 and 2 you can make 26, 63, 3, 263 ...

Now write them in order.

Key words

digits

Quick Test

1. The first bead is yellow. What colour is the fifth bead?

2. Which number is bigger: 54 or 45?

3. Which number is halfway between 6 and 14?

4. Write these numbers in order, starting with the smallest: 24, 38, 19, 32, 27.

5. What number comes after 97?

Estimating

Good estimates

Estimating is a bit like guessing. It is better than a guess though – particularly if you are good with numbers.

Have a quick look at this pile of buttons. Without counting, estimate approximately how many buttons there are.

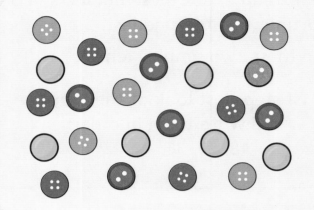

Now count them. There are 25 altogether – but your estimate would be good if you thought there was anything between 20 and 30. **An estimate does not need to be exact**. It is a good idea to roughly count them in groups of 5 or 10 – you can do this quite quickly.

Try this with handfuls of buttons or counters and see how good your estimates are.

Number lines

You might be asked to estimate the position of a point on a line. For example, estimate the number marked by the arrow.

0   10

The best way to do this is to **find the approximate halfway position**. You can then count on to work out the number. In the picture above, the arrow is just past the halfway point, which is 5, so it points, approximately, to the number 6.

Rounding

Rounding a number to the nearest ten is useful for estimating. **A round number is a number ending in zero:** 10, 20, 30, 40, 50, 60, 70, 80, 90 or 100.

Rounding is easy if you follow these two simple rules:

To round to the nearest 10 look at the 'ones' digit:

1   **If it is 5 or more, round up the tens digit.**

2   **If it is less than 5, the tens digit stays the same.**

54 rounds down to 50

38 rounds up to 40

65 rounds up to 70

The halfway numbers like 65, 45, 85, 25... always round up to the next ten.

Have a go...

Play an estimating game in pairs.
- *One player takes a handful of buttons or beads and gives an estimate of the number taken.*
- *The other player says 'higher' or 'lower', if they think the actual number is different from the estimate.*
- *Count the buttons to find the winner.*
- *Swap over and repeat the game.*

Top Tip

Remember, a number is always between two possible 'round' numbers – you just have to choose which one it is nearest to.

Key words

estimate   rounding

approximate

Quick Test

0 |————A↓————B↓—| 20

1 What number is the arrow A pointing to?

2 What number is the arrow B pointing to?

3 What is 74 rounded to the nearest 10?

4 What is 45 rounded to the nearest 10?

5 Approximately how many words are there in this quick test?

Fractions

What is a fraction?

A **fraction** is **part of a whole**.

One-quarter ($\frac{1}{4}$) means 1 part taken out of 4 equal pieces.

So if you want to eat $\frac{1}{4}$ of a pizza, you can cut the pizza into four equal pieces and take one of the pieces. This leaves $\frac{3}{4}$ (three-quarters) for somebody else.

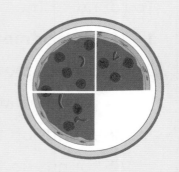

Fractions of shapes

Try to learn these different fractions:

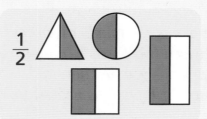

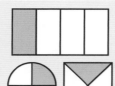

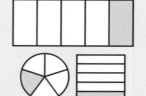

Remember – the bottom number of a fraction shows the number of equal parts. The top number shows how many are taken.

Equal parts

Look at the blue shape. Do you think it is divided into four quarters?

No, they are not quarters. It is in four parts but the parts are not equal. Shapes cut in quarters are in **four equal parts**.

Fractions of amounts

It is easy to find one-half or one-quarter of different amounts, as long as you know how to divide.

Here are 12 sweets.

To find $\frac{1}{2}$ of 12, divide the sweets into **two equal groups** and count one of the groups.

So $\frac{1}{2}$ of 12 = 12 ÷ 2 = 6.

To find $\frac{1}{4}$ of 12, divide the sweets into **four equal groups** and count one of the groups.

So $\frac{1}{4}$ of 12 = 12 ÷ 4 = 3.

To find three-quarters ($\frac{3}{4}$) of 12, divide the sweets into four equal groups and count three of the groups.

So $\frac{3}{4}$ of 12 = 12 ÷ 4 = 3

Then 3 × 3 = 9

Did you know that two halves make a whole?

I hope nobody falls in!

Have a go...

You will need a pile of coins or buttons.
Take a handful and try to find $\frac{1}{2}$ or $\frac{1}{4}$ of the amount by counting them out. Some will be impossible, but write down the ones that you can divide equally. For example, $\frac{1}{2}$ of 6 = 3.

Key words

fraction

Quick Test

1 What fraction of this square is red?

2 Is this circle divided into halves?

3 What is $\frac{1}{2}$ of 10?

4 What is $\frac{1}{4}$ of 8?

5 What is $\frac{1}{4}$ of 20?

Test your skills

Abacus numbers

You need: 5 counters, buttons or pennies.

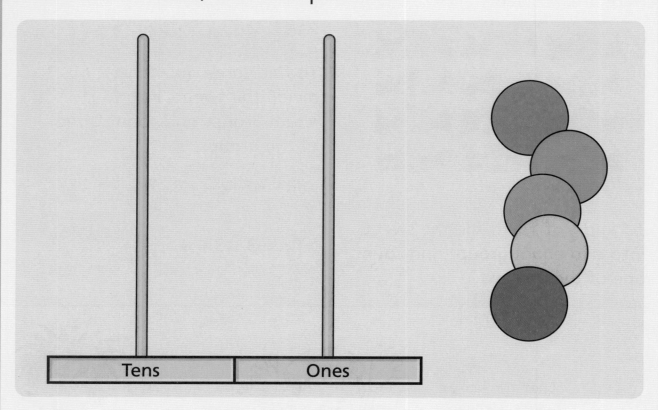

Use one counter and place it on this abacus to make different numbers.

You can make 1 or 10 with one counter.

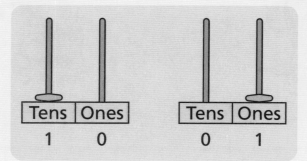

Which different numbers can you make with two counters? What about 3, 4, 5... counters?

More numbers

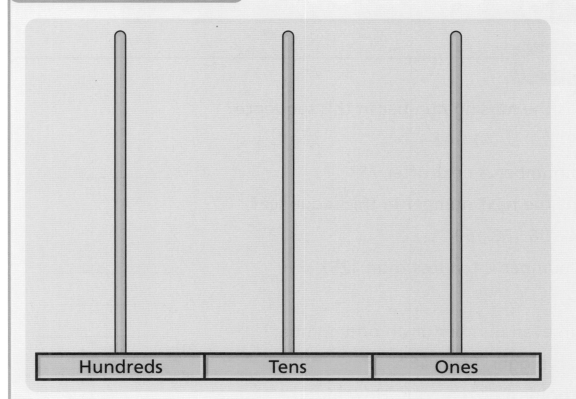

Hundreds	Tens	Ones

You can make three different numbers with one counter on this abacus.

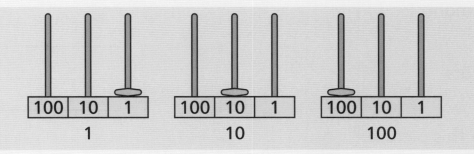

How many different numbers can you make with two counters?

What about 3, 4, 5... counters?

Keep a list of all the numbers and write them in order of size.

Aren't those my pennies?

Hands off, you've spent your pocket money! Ask Mum for some buttons!

Test your knowledge

Section 1

1 What is the missing number in this sequence?

   38 39 ____ 41 42

2 Which number is next after 75? _____

3 What is the next number in this sequence?

   52 54 56 58 60 ____

4 What number is ten less than 125? _____

5 8 − 0 = ? _____

6 Is 56 an even number or an odd number? _____

7 Which is bigger, 84 or 48? _____

8 A box holds a dozen eggs. How many
   eggs are there? _____

9 Count how many:

   a flowers _____

   b caterpillars _____

   c bees _____

   there are in this picture.

Section 2

1   What fraction of each of these shapes is red?

a   b   c

_____   _____   _____

2   What number is 10 more than 62?   _____

3   What is 16 rounded to the nearest 10?   _____

4   What number is halfway between 18 and 22?   _____

5   What number between 35 and 45 is a multiple of 10?   _____

6   Is 20 a multiple of both 2 and 5?   _____

7   What number is the arrow pointing to?

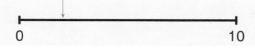

_____

Section 3

1   What is $\frac{3}{4}$ of 16?   _____

2   A cake cut in half will be cut into 4 equal pieces. True or false?   _____

3   What number is this?   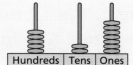   _____

4   The train is pulling 6 carriages. The first is carrying a horse.

a   Which carriage has an elephant?   _____

b   What animal is in the 5th carriage?   _____

c   What is in the 2nd carriage?   _____

Number facts

Totals to 10

Try to learn all these facts for the different **totals**. Use these four steps to help you:

1 look at them

2 cover them up

3 say the facts

4 check the facts

$0 + 1 = \boxed{1}$

$\left.\begin{array}{l} 0 + 2 \\ 1 + 1 \end{array}\right\} = \boxed{2}$

$\left.\begin{array}{l} 0 + 3 \\ 1 + 2 \end{array}\right\} = \boxed{3}$

$\left.\begin{array}{l} 0 + 4 \\ 1 + 3 \\ 2 + 2 \end{array}\right\} = \boxed{4}$

$\left.\begin{array}{l} 0 + 5 \\ 1 + 4 \\ 2 + 3 \end{array}\right\} = \boxed{5}$

$\left.\begin{array}{l} 0 + 6 \\ 1 + 5 \\ 2 + 4 \\ 3 + 3 \end{array}\right\} = \boxed{6}$

$\left.\begin{array}{l} 0 + 7 \\ 1 + 6 \\ 2 + 5 \\ 3 + 4 \end{array}\right\} = \boxed{7}$

$\left.\begin{array}{l} 0 + 8 \\ 1 + 7 \\ 2 + 6 \\ 3 + 5 \\ 4 + 4 \end{array}\right\} = \boxed{8}$

$\left.\begin{array}{l} 0 + 9 \\ 1 + 8 \\ 2 + 7 \\ 3 + 6 \\ 4 + 5 \end{array}\right\} = \boxed{9}$

$\left.\begin{array}{l} 0 + 10 \\ 1 + 9 \\ 2 + 8 \\ 3 + 7 \\ 4 + 6 \\ 5 + 5 \end{array}\right\} = \boxed{10}$

Trios

$8 - 5 = 3$ is a subtraction fact. The subtraction facts to 10 are easy to remember, if you know your addition facts.

$3 + 5 = 8$
and
$5 + 3 = 8$

These are two addition facts and you can use them to work out two subtraction facts:

$8 - 5 = 3$
and
$8 - 3 = 5$

The three numbers 8, 5 and 3 are called a trio.
They can make four addition and subtraction facts.

Think of some more trios and the facts you can make from them.

Number bonds

Try to learn all your **number bonds** to 20. These are the **addition and subtraction facts up to 20**, such as 7 + 8, 16 − 9 and so on.

	0	1	2	3	4	5	6	7	8	9	10
0	0	1	2	3	4	5	6	7	8	9	10
1	1	2	3	4	5	6	7	8	9	10	11
2	2	3	4	5	6	7	8	9	10	11	12
3	3	4	5	6	7	8	9	10	11	12	13
4	4	5	6	7	8	9	10	11	12	13	14
5	5	6	7	8	9	10	11	12	13	14	15
6	6	7	8	9	10	11	12	13	14	15	16
7	7	8	9	10	11	12	13	14	15	16	17
8	8	9	10	11	12	13	14	15	16	17	18
9	9	10	11	12	13	14	15	16	17	18	19
10	10	11	12	13	14	15	16	17	18	19	20

3 + 9 = 12
9 + 3 = 12
12 − 3 = 9
12 − 9 = 3

This table contains all the facts. Use it to practise and learn the ones you cannot do quickly.

Top Tip

Remember that 4 + 6 gives the same answer as 6 + 4. It does not matter which way round you add.

Close your eyes and count up to 20.

1,2,3,4,5,6,7... and 13 is 20! Coming to find you!

Have a go...

• *Use number cards 1 to 20 and pick out different trios, such as 4, 5, 9 or 3, 8, 11.*

• *Write down the four addition and subtraction facts for each trio.*

Key words

total	number bonds

Quick Test

Answer these as quickly as you can.

1. 3 + 5
2. 4 + 6
3. 2 + 9
4. 4 + 8
5. 7 + 7
6. 6 − 4
7. 9 − 5
8. 11 − 8
9. 14 − 6
10. 15 − 11

Addition and subtraction

Big numbers

If you know a fact such as **3 + 6 = 9**, you can use this to work out:

> 30 + 60   300 + 600   3000 + 6000 etc.

You can also work out **23 + 6**, which is **20 + 3 + 6**.

So you can see that knowing your number bonds to 20 is very useful.

Using doubles

Doubles of numbers can be quite easy to work out – so **use them to work out other near-doubles**.

Examples: 6 + 6 = 12 so 6 + 7 is 1 more, which is 13.

20 + 20 = 40 so 20 + 21 is 1 more, which is 41.

Rounding

If you need to add or take away 9, round it to 10 to make it easier.

Examples: 7 + 9   7 add 10, take away 1   Answer: 16.

14 – 9   14 take away 10, add 1   Answer: 5.

You can use this method to add or take away 19, 29, 39, 49...

Top Tip

If you are asked to add or subtract numbers, always look at the numbers carefully before deciding on the best method to use.

Adding 2-digit numbers

If you need to add two big numbers, it helps to **break the numbers up and add the tens, then the ones**.

Example:

25 + 37

Use these three steps:

1 Hold the bigger number in your head: 37.

2 Add the tens: 37 + 20 = 57.

3 Add the ones: 57 + 5 = 62.

Counting on

A really good method for subtraction is to **find the difference between the numbers by counting on**.

Example: 34 – 18

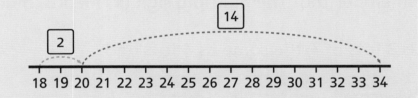

This number line shows exactly what goes on in your head.

Count on from 18 to 20, then on to 34. 14 + 2 is 16, so 34 – 18 = 16.

Have a go...

Put 10 or 12 different coins in a bag. Take out a handful of the coins and work out the total. Is it more or less than 50p? How much less than £1 is it?

Key words

difference

Quick Test

Work out the answers to these:

1 60 + 50

2 The sum of 12 and 13

3 27 take away 9

4 16 + 25

5 What is the difference between 33 and 18?

Multiplication and division

Counting groups

When you **multiply** something, you make it larger – and counting groups is a good way of working out a multiplication.

There are 4 fish swimming in each bowl.

How many fish are there altogether in 3 bowls?

3 lots of 4 is the same as 4 + 4 + 4, which is 12.

This means 4 multiplied by 3, or 4 × 3 = 12

Remember that **the multiply sign (×) means 'multiplied by'**.

Is 3 lots of 4 the same as 4 lots of 3?

The answer is the same, but the fish have a bit more room in their bowls!

If you put the fish together you can see that 4 × 3 is the same as 3 × 4.

This is important to remember:

4 × 3   =   3 × 4

5 × 2   =   2 × 5

3 × 10   =   10 × 3

The answers are the same written both ways.

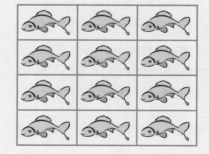

Top Tip

If you have a division sum to work out, such as 20 ÷ 5, turn it into a multiplication: 5 times something makes 20. If you know your 5× table, you can then work it out: 5 × 4 = 20, so 20 ÷ 5 = 4.

Dividing

Dividing **is the opposite of multiplying** – it is the **same as sharing or grouping**. Both these pictures show 15 divided by 3.

15 shells are shared between 3. There are 5 in each group.
15 ÷ 3 = 5

15 shells are grouped into 3s. There are 5 groups. 15 ÷ 3 = 5

Whichever way you look at it, you can see how it fits with multiplying:

3 × 5 = 15   5 × 3 = 15   15 ÷ 3 = 5   15 ÷ 5 = 3

15, 5 and 3 are **a special set of three numbers called a trio**.

If I share these 6 sweets between us, I get 4 and you get 2.

That's not half!

I never said I'd share them *equally*!

Have a go...

Use a calculator to explore multiplication patterns.

Press the keys ②➕➕*, then* ﹦﹦﹦*.*

Continue this to see the pattern for counting in 2s. Explore other patterns by changing the 2 to 3, 4, 5 or any other number.

Key words

multiply   divide

Quick Test

1 If there are 4 stickers in a packet, how many would there be in 4 packets?

2 Does 3 multiplied by 5 give the same answer as 5 multiplied by 3?

3 What is double 14?

4 What is half of 12?

5 What is 12 divided by 4?

Times tables

2 times table

All the numbers in the 2 times table are **even numbers**. Here is the full set up to 2 × 10:

2 × 1 = 2	2 × 3 = 6	2 × 5 = 10	2 × 7 = 14	2 × 9 = 18
2 × 2 = 4	2 × 4 = 8	2 × 6 = 12	2 × 8 = 16	2 × 10 = 20

They look easy when they are written in order like this – but you need to know each of these facts off by heart.

Write down any that you are not sure of and try to learn them. **Use other facts to help you**.

Example: If you cannot remember that 2 × 6 is 12, just say 2 × 5 is 10 and 2 more is 12.

Top Tip

Remember that 2 × 6 gives the same answer as 6 × 2 – it does not matter which way round it is written.

Multiplying by 5 and 10

These are the easiest tables to learn because of their patterns:

• numbers in the 5 × table always end in 5 or 0.

• numbers in the 10 × table always end in 0.

5 × 1 = 5	5 × 3 = 15	5 × 5 = 25	5 × 7 = 35	5 × 9 = 45
5 × 2 = 10	5 × 4 = 20	5 × 6 = 30	5 × 8 = 40	5 × 10 = 50

Have you noticed that when it is 5 times an odd number the answer ends in 5, and when it is 5 times an even number the answer ends in 0?

10 × 1 = 10	10 × 3 = 30	10 × 5 = 50	10 × 7 = 70	10 × 9 = 90
10 × 2 = 20	10 × 4 = 40	10 × 6 = 60	10 × 8 = 80	10 × 10 = 100

Look at these and cover each answer up with your finger. Are there any that you do not know really quickly?

Multiplying by 3 and 4

3 × 1 = 3	4 × 1 = 4
3 × 2 = 6	4 × 2 = 8
3 × 3 = 9	4 × 3 = 12
3 × 4 = 12	4 × 4 = 16
3 × 5 = 15	4 × 5 = 20
3 × 6 = 18	4 × 6 = 24
3 × 7 = 21	4 × 7 = 28
3 × 8 = 24	4 × 8 = 32
3 × 9 = 27	4 × 9 = 36
3 × 10 = 30	4 × 10 = 40

These are a bit trickier and there may be some you do not know. Don't panic – use the facts you do know to help learn the others.

Examples:

- 3 × 8 is **double** 3 × 4. Double 12 is 24.
- 3 × 9 is 3 less than 3 × 10, so it is 27.
- 4 × 7 is double 2 × 7. Double 14 is 28.

Tricky tables

These are the facts for the tables that probably cause the most problems:

3 × 6 = 18	3 × 7 = 21	3 × 9 = 27	4 × 6 = 24
9 × 8 = 72	4 × 9 = 36	3 × 8 = 24	4 × 7 = 28

Learn one fact a day. Try this: every time you go through a doorway at home, say the fact out loud.

Have a go...

Ask someone to give you a tables test.
- *Write 20 tables facts down on paper to read out.*
- *Record your time and score.*
- *Try to beat your best time and score.*

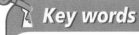

Key words

even numbers   double

Quick Test

Answer these as quickly as you can:

1. 3 × 4
2. 5 × 6
3. 10 × 7
4. 4 × 4
5. 9 × 2
6. 5 × 4
7. 4 × 8
8. 10 × 3
9. 2 × 7
10. 3 × 9

Problem-solving

Word problems

Many test questions are disguised as tricky word problems. When you see one, don't panic, just follow the four steps.

Example: A pet shop has 15 hamsters for sale. On Monday, 3 hamsters are sold. On the following day, another 5 hamsters are sold. How many hamsters does the shop have left to sell on Wednesday?

Step 1: Read the problem
Try to picture the problem and imagine it in real life.

Step 2: Sort out the calculations
It is 15 take away 3 and then take away another 5.

Step 3: Answer the calculations
15 − 3 = 12   12 − 5 = 7

Step 4: Answer the problem
Look back at the question – what is it asking?

Answer: There are 7 hamsters left for sale.

Money totals

When you are finding **totals** of a set of coins, **always start with the highest-value coins first**. Then you can add the smallest coins.

Example:

Find the total:

50p + 20p +10p + 2p + 2p + 1p = 85p

Giving change

When shopkeepers give change, they **count on from the price of the item up to the amount of money given**.

Example:

This card costs 37p.

What change will there be from 50p?

37p

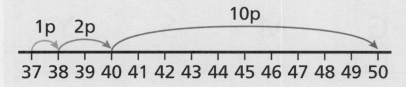

10p

1p   2p

37 38 39 40 41 42 43 44 45 46 47 48 49 50

37p up to 38p is   1

38p up to 40p is   2

40p up to 50p is 10

So the change given is 1p + 2p + 10p, which is 13p.

Try this method, giving change from £1.

Top Tip

Remember that the £ is a 'pound' sign and the 'point' in £4.59 separates the pounds (£4) from the pence (59p). Be careful with zeros: £2.05 means £2 and 5p and £2.50 means £2 and 50p.

Have a go...

Explain to someone:

* *The four steps for solving word problems.*

* *How to give change from £1 for different items. Use coins to demonstrate the shopkeeper's method of counting on to give change.*

Key words

total

Quick Test

1 There are 12 tennis balls to put in some tubes. If 3 balls fit in each tube, how many tubes are needed?

2 Kim has 25p and Adam has 10p more than Kim. How much have they got altogether?

3 Rhian has three 10p coins, a 50p coin and two 5p coins in her purse. How much has she got in total?

4 A doughnut costs 34p. What change will there be from 50p?

5 Pencils cost 40p each. Alex has £1. How much more money does he need to buy three pencils?

Test your skills

Coin Alphabet

Coin Alphabet is a game where you replace the letters in words with numbers. This grid tells you what each letter is worth.

1p	A	G	M	S	Y
2p	B	H	N	T	Z
5p	C	I	O	U	
10p	D	J	P	V	
20p	E	K	Q	W	
50p	F	L	R	X	

Sam is worth 1p + 1p + 1p : a total of 3p.

Paul is worth 10p + 1p + 5p + 50p : a total of 66p.

What is your name worth?

More to try

Investigate different boys' and girls' names.

- Can you find any names that are worth the same? For example, Sam and Amy are both worth 3p.

- Which 4-letter name is worth the most?
  Which is worth the least?

- Which is the most expensive name you can find?

- Can you find any names that are worth exactly £1?
  Could you find two names that total £1?

I'm worth 71p!

That's not fair! I'm only worth 3p!

Test your knowledge

Section 1

1 What is the difference between 20 and 13?   _____

2 600 + 500 =   _____

3 What is the sum of 50 and 51?   _____

4 There are 5 pencils in a pack.
   How many pencils are there in 4 packs?   _____

5 8 × 3 =   _____

6 A cat had 8 kittens. 3 were tabby, 1 was white and
   the rest were black. How many kittens were black?   _____

7 What is 12 less than 30?   _____

8 60 ÷ 10 =   _____

9 What is the total of these coins?

_____

10 How much will it cost to buy:

       a 10 flags   _____

       b a bucket and a flag   _____

       c a bucket and a spade   _____

Section 2

1 Take away 9 from 34. _____

2 26 + 15 = _____

3 Kate has £1. She buys an ice-cream for 65p.
How much money does she have left? _____

4 What is 35 divided by 5? _____

5 What is double 30? _____

6 4 children divide 20 sweets.
How many sweets do they each get? _____

7 What is half of 40? _____

8 9 × 3 = _____

Section 3

1 a How many bags of crisps are there
altogether in the multipacks? _____

 b How many chocolate bars are there in total? _____

 c How many more packets of crisps are
there than chocolate bars? _____

2 I am thinking of a number. If I subtract 11 the answer is 5.
What number am I thinking of?

_____

2-D shapes

Shape names

2-D means 2-dimensional. 2-dimensional shapes are flat shapes. There are lots of 2-D shapes, all with long and interesting names. It is important to be able to recognise these shapes and know their names.

Number of sides	Name	
3	Triangle	
4	Quadrilateral	
5	Pentagon	
6	Hexagon	
7	Heptagon	
8	Octagon	

If you see a shape and do not know its name, just count the number of sides.

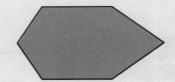

This is a 6-sided shape. A six-sided shape is called a hexagon.

Regular shapes are special shapes with all sides and angles equal.

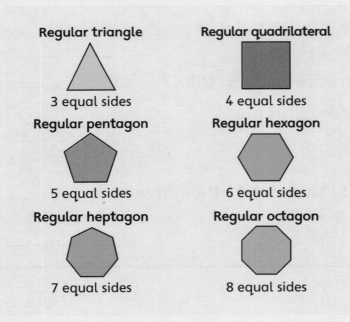

Regular triangle
3 equal sides

Regular quadrilateral
4 equal sides

Regular pentagon
5 equal sides

Regular hexagon
6 equal sides

Regular heptagon
7 equal sides

Regular octagon
8 equal sides

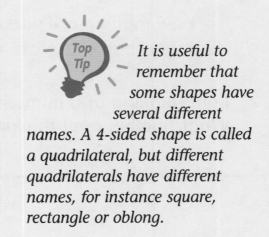

It is useful to remember that some shapes have several different names. A 4-sided shape is called a quadrilateral, but different quadrilaterals have different names, for instance square, rectangle or oblong.

Sorting shapes

A **Venn diagram** (see p. 48) is useful for sorting shapes.

A circle and an oval have one curved side so they are in the outside set.

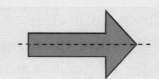

Symmetry

Some shapes are **symmetrical** – they have lines of symmetry. Look at this shape:

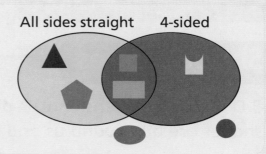

If you imagine it folded down the middle, the two sides would match. That fold line is the line of symmetry and shows that a shape or pattern is symmetrical.

A B C D

These letters are symmetrical. Can you see where the lines of symmetry would be?

Have a go...

Play the feely bag game with someone.

- *Cut different shapes out of thick card.*

- *Put them in a bag and shake them up.*

- *Feel one of the shapes through the bag and describe it – can the other person name it from your description?*

Key words

Venn diagram   symmetrical

Quick Test

1. What is the name of a six-sided shape?

2. How many sides does a pentagon have?

3. Which shape has four equal sides and angles?

4. Is this triangle symmetrical?

5. What is the name of any shape with 4 sides?

6. Which shape has more sides – a heptagon or an octagon?

3-D solids

Shape names

3-D means 3-dimensional. 3-dimensional shapes are solid shapes. Solid shapes are all around us and many of them have special names.

Try this: Look at one shape and remember its name.

- Close your eyes and picture the shape floating on the back of your eyelids.

- Turn the shape around and try to picture it with different parts facing you.

- Try this with other shapes so that you really get to know them.

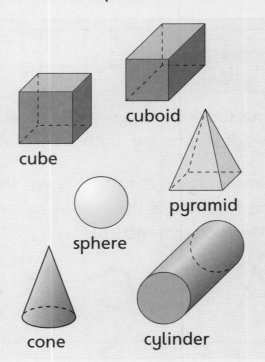

cube

cuboid

pyramid

sphere

cone

cylinder

Parts of solid shapes

Solid shapes are made up of faces, edges and corners.

A face is a flat surface of a solid. An edge is where two faces meet. A corner is where three or more edges meet.

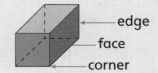

edge

face

corner

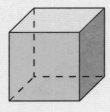

A cube has 6 faces, 12 edges and 8 corners.

A cylinder has 3 faces (2 flat and 1 curved), 2 edges and no corners.

Check the faces, edges and corners of other shapes.

Sorting shapes

You can sort shapes using a **Carroll diagram** (see p. 48).

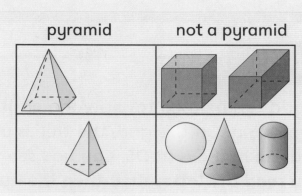

	pyramid	not a pyramid
one or more square faces		
no square faces		

Shapes all around us

These solid shapes that you are learning about make up a lot of the shapes that are all around you. It is important to be able to recognise and name the shapes. Go on a shape hunt and see how many cubes, cuboids, spheres, cylinders, cones and pyramids you can find.

I think a cone is my favourite.

Me too - with strawberry ice-cream!

Have a go...

• Find some 3-D shapes from packets and boxes around the house.

• List the number of faces, edges and corners they have.

Key words

face

edge

corner

Carroll diagram

Quick Test

1 Which shape has 6 square faces and 8 corners?

2 How many faces does a cylinder have?

3 What is the name of the shape that is absolutely round like a ball?

4 What is this shape called?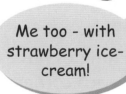

5 Name two solid shapes that have circle faces.

Position and turning

Grids

A grid can be used to show the position of something. On this grid, the tree is at C3 and the house is at D5. Can you see that you **read the letter first, then the number, to give the position**?

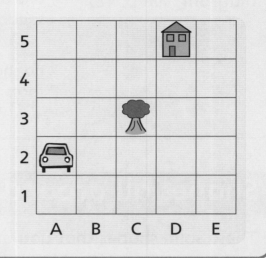

Right angles

Corners of doors, windows, books and tables all show right angles.

These are 'square' angles and can be seen all around us.

A right angle is a quarter turn, clockwise or anti-clockwise.

Squares and rectangles have four right angles – one at each corner.

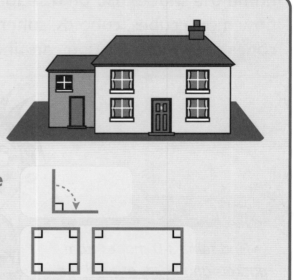

Points of the compass

It is useful to know the points of the compass.

To remember the order, look at the initials NESW. A well-known saying to learn this order is **Naughty Elephants Squirt Water!**

Can you think up any of your own?

Directions

Clockwise and anti-clockwise are instructions for moving in different directions.

This direction is clockwise.

This is anti-clockwise

Quarter turns, half turns and whole turns are used to describe how far to turn.

This arrow has moved a quarter turn clockwise.

This arrow has moved a half turn anti-clockwise.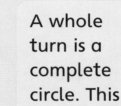

A whole turn is a complete circle. This is a whole turn clockwise.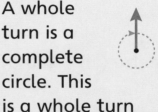

 Top Tip *Remember, clockwise is in the direction of clock hands, and anti-clockwise is in the opposite direction.*

Have a go...

Set a course for someone to walk through. Use clockwise, anti-clockwise, left, right, quarter turns and half turns for direction. Use steps for distance.

🔑 Key words

right angle   anti-clockwise
clockwise   square

Quick Test

1 What position on the grid is the car on page 38?

2 Which compass direction is opposite west?

3 Which point will the arrow move to if it makes a quarter turn anti-clockwise?

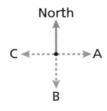

North

C ◄----•----► A

B

4 Which point will the arrow move to if it makes a half turn clockwise?

5 Which compass direction is opposite south?

Measurement

Units of measurement

Length, mass and capacity are all measured using different units. Try to learn these:

Capacity
1 litre (l) = 1000 millilitres (ml)

Mass
1 kilogram (kg) = 1000 grams (g)

Length
1 metre (m) = 100 cm   1 kilometre (km) = 1000 m

It is important to write the units in your answers. Which units of measurement do you think would be correct on these labels? Check your answers by looking in your kitchen cupboards.

Heavier or lighter?

We measure mass using grams and kilograms. To help you get an idea of these masses, look at these. They are all approximate amounts:

1 gram – a pinch of salt

100 grams – an apple

20 grams – a teaspoon of sugar

1000 grams or 1 kg – a bag of sugar

Try to get a feel for these masses by holding different objects and 'weighing' them in your hands.

Longer or shorter?

We measure the length of objects using a ruler or tape measure. Before you measure something, however, it is a good idea to work out roughly how long it is. This is called **estimating**.

Example: Is your shoe longer or shorter than 10 cm? You need to know how long 10 cm is to work this out.

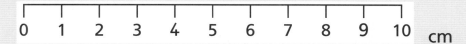

cm

Look at different objects and estimate whether they are longer or shorter than 10 cm. Try comparing objects with 30 cm, 50 cm and 1 metre.

I think this bucket holds about 5 litres.

Top Tip A handspan is about 10 cm long, so use this to work out the approximate length of objects by counting in tens.

 Have a go...

Play an estimating weight game called 'higher or lower' with someone.

• Choose an object, pick it up and 'weigh' it in your hands.

• Estimate the mass in grams or kilograms. The other person then says whether they think the real mass is higher or lower than the estimate.

• Use some scales to see who was correct. Take turns to estimate and weigh.

I estimate that's just enough to get you absolutely soaked!

Key words

length · approximate
mass · estimate
capacity · weight

Quick Test

1 How many millilitres are there in 1 litre?

2 A door in a house is usually about 2 metres high. True or false?

3 Approximately how heavy is a pencil – 20 g or 200 g?

4 What is measured in kilograms – length, mass or capacity?

5 How many centimetres are there in $1\frac{1}{2}$ metres?

Time

Time facts

There are lots of time facts to try to learn. Cover each one up and see how many you know.

60 seconds = 1 minute

1 day = 24 hours

1 week = 7 days

Sun.	Mon	Tues	Wed	Thur	Fri	Sat

60 minutes = 1 hour

1 year = 12 months = 365 days

leap year = 366 days

Spring   Summer

Winter   Autumn

Use the 'knuckle method' to learn the number of days in the months:

All the 'knuckle months' have 31 days. February has 28 days (29 days in a leap year) and April, June, September and November have 30 days.

Jan Mar May Jul
Feb Apr Jun

Aug Oct Dec
Sep Nov

Top Tip

Put a calendar up in your bedroom so you can mark off the days for each month. You will soon get to know the order of the days in the week and the months in the year.

Reading the time

We read the time using these two types of clock:

an analogue clock **with hands**

the long hand shows how many minutes past the hour

the short hand shows the hour

a digital clock **with the time shown in numbers**

shows the hour

shows how many minutes past

Both these clocks show 'four fifteen', or '15 minutes past 4'.

If you find it difficult to tell the time, then follow these three easy steps:

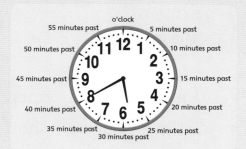

1 Start with the short hour hand on your clock or watch. Look at the last hour that this has gone past. On this clock, the short hand has gone past the 5, so it is past 5 o'clock.

2 Look at the longer minute hand and count around in fives from the top to the hand: 5, 10, 15, 20, 25, 30, 35, 40.

3 Say aloud the hour followed by the number of minutes – so you say 5:40, which means 40 minutes past 5.

Have a go...

Ask someone to write down a digital time, such as 2:45.

Use an old watch or clock and try to make that time by turning the hands.

Key words

analogue clock

digital clock

Quick Test

1 How many minutes are there in 1 hour?

2 Which day comes after Wednesday?

3 Which month comes before October?

4 What time does this show?

5 What will the time on this clock be in 15 minutes?

Test your skills

Shape parts

This is a half-shape.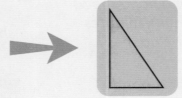

The whole shape could be one of these.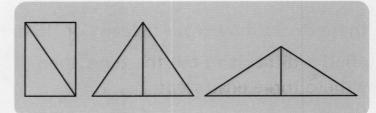

- Use thin card or paper.
- Cut out your own 'half-shapes'.
- Find all the whole shapes that can be made from your half.
- You could choose one of these half-shapes.

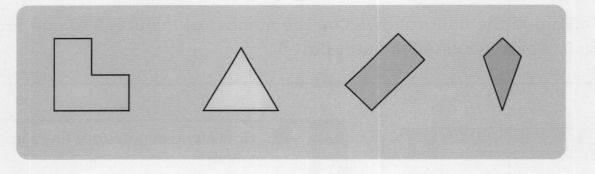

Top Tip

Keep the starting shape simple and then try to find as many different complete shapes as you can. There may be lots!

Bigger shapes

This is a quarter of a shape.

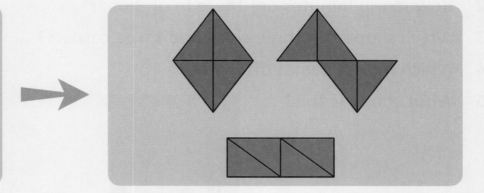

The whole shape could be one of these.

- Make your own 'quarter-shapes'.

- Find the different whole shapes that you can make from your quarter-shape.

- Make a set of whole shapes and glue them on a piece of paper to display them. You could colour them in if you like!

I think I've found a quarter of a footprint.

Maybe it was someone walking on tiptoes!

Test your knowledge

Section 1

1 What is the name of a five-sided shape? _____

2 How many minutes are there in an hour? _____

3 Which shape has three sides and three corners? _____

4 Which month comes after July? _____

5 What shape is this?

_____

6 How many faces does a cube have? _____

7 What number is opposite 3 on a clock face? _____

8 Is a square symmetrical? _____

9 What is the time on each of these clocks?

a    b    c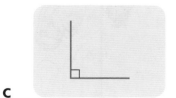

_____   _____   _____

10 Which of these is a right angle? _____

a   b   c

Section 2

1   Which compass point is opposite south?   _____

2
How much does the parcel weigh?

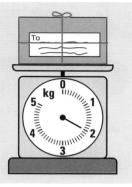

_____

3   What units would you use to measure a glass of orange juice: centimetres, grams or millilitres?   _____

4   Measure this line with a ruler. Is it nearest to 5 cm, 6 cm or 7 cm?

_____

5   A banana is heavier than 1 kg. True or false?   _____

6   Which is the same amount as 1 litre?

10 ml   100 ml   1000 ml   _____

7   If you are facing north and you do a quarter turn clockwise, what direction will you be facing?   _____

8   Which object is to the left of the bucket on the grid?

_____

9   Which object is south of the sandcastle?

_____

10 Which objects are at

a C4   _____

b A1   _____

c D2   _____

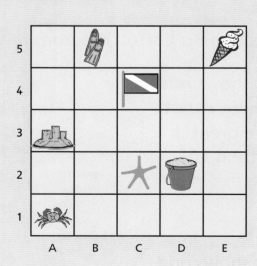

Sorting diagrams

Venn diagrams

If you wanted to sort these shapes into two groups, red shapes and triangles, you could **use a** Venn diagram.

This shows shapes that are not red or triangles

This shows the set of red shapes

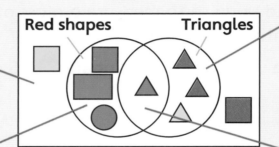

This shows the set of triangles

This shows red shapes that are triangles

Carroll diagrams

Carroll diagrams are very similar to Venn diagrams, **except they use a grid rather than circles.**

You can use a Carroll diagram to sort numbers.

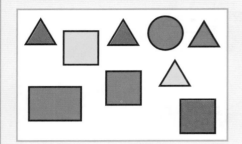

This shows odd numbers that are greater than 10

This shows numbers that are greater than 10 and not odd

	odd numbers	not odd numbers
greater than 10	15 17 13 19	14 12 20
not greater than 10	3 9	6

This shows odd numbers that are less than 10

This shows numbers that are less than 10 and not odd

Tree diagrams

A **tree diagram** is a good way of sorting things by asking questions. Each of the answers is either yes or no.

You can use tree diagrams to sort shapes, numbers or objects. This tree diagram sorts some fruit.

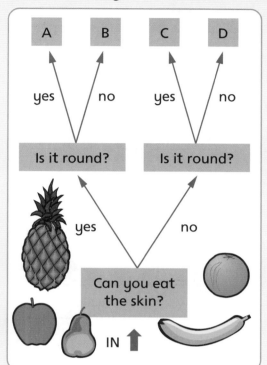

Example: Start with the banana and follow the questions through the tree diagram.

Can you eat the skin of a banana? No

Is a banana round? No

So a banana ends up in box D.

Which boxes do the other fruits in this section go into?

Have a go...

Use the labels from the Carroll diagram: odd numbers/not odd numbers and greater than 10/ not greater than 10.

Sort the numbers to 20 using these labels on a Venn diagram and then a tree diagram.

Compare each of the ways of sorting.

Key words

Venn diagram   odd numbers

Carrol diagram   tree diagram

Quick Test

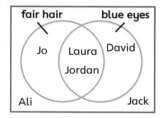

From this Venn diagram, name someone who has:

1 Blue eyes and fair hair

2 Blue eyes but not fair hair

3 Neither fair hair nor blue eyes

4 Fair hair but not blue eyes

49

Pictograms and graphs

Pictograms

Pictograms use symbols or pictures, where **each symbol represents a certain number of items**.

This pictogram shows how many jelly babies are in a box.

Look carefully at what each picture stands for. Each picture represents 2 jelly babies, so for instance, there are 9 purple jelly babies in the box. Count to check.

How many red jelly babies are there? You should have counted 6.

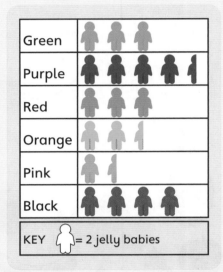

The pictogram below shows the hours of sunshine each week for 6 weeks.

For this pictogram, each sun stands for 5 hours of sunshine. So in week one, there were between 15 and 20 hours of sunshine.

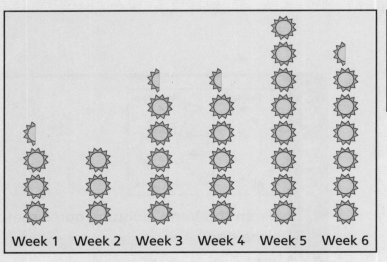

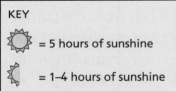

Block graphs

This type of **block graph** is the easiest type of graph, because **each block shows one thing**. As with all graphs, however, you still need to look at it carefully.

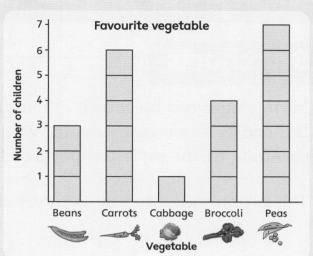

Favourite vegetable

Which is the most popular vegetable? You can see that peas are the most popular: 7 children chose them.

How many more children liked broccoli than cabbage? This is a typical question. Work out both amounts and then find the difference. 4 children liked broccoli, 1 child liked cabbage. 4 − 1 is 3. So the difference is 3.

You can work out how many children were in the group altogether by counting all the blocks.

I'm amazed that someone chose cabbage as their favourite vegetable.

Actually it was me! Nicer than your mushy peas!

Have a go...

• Carry out a survey of your family's favourite fruit or vegetables.

• Draw a pictogram or block graph to show your results.

Key words

pictogram   block graph

Quick Test

Use the graphs on these pages to answer these questions:

1 How many more black jelly babies are there in the box than green ones?

2 Which two colours had the same number of jelly babies?

3 How many hours of sunshine were there in week 2?

4 In which week were there 17 hours of sunshine?

5 How many children chose beans as their favourite vegetable?

Graphs and charts

Bar charts

Information can be shown in many ways. Using different graphs and bar charts is one very popular way. To understand bar charts, look carefully at the different parts of this graph.

This graph shows the birds that visited a bird table.

1 **Work out the** scale – look carefully at the numbers – do they go up in 1s, 2s, 5s, 10s ... ?

2 **Read the title** – what is it all about? Is there any other information given?

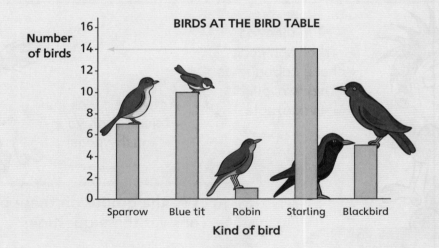

BIRDS AT THE BIRD TABLE

Number of birds

Kind of bird

3 **Look at the** axis labels – these should explain the lines that go up and across

4 **Compare the bars** – read them across to work out the amounts.

The scale is very important. This graph goes up in 2s. You can see that the number of sparrows is halfway between 6 and 8 – so there were 7 sparrows visiting the bird table.

Changing scales

This graph has a scale that goes up in fives.

Jack measured the height of the flowers in his flowerbed.

Use the graph to check the different heights of the flowers.

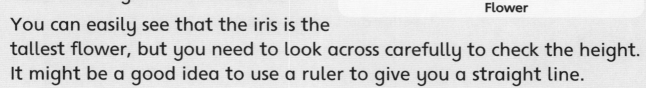

Jack's flowers

You can easily see that the iris is the tallest flower, but you need to look across carefully to check the height. It might be a good idea to use a ruler to give you a straight line.

A common test question would be something like:

How much taller is the lily than the poppy?

All you need to do is find the height of each flower and work out the difference. The lily is 34 cm and the poppy is 18 cm.

34 − 18 = 16, so the lily is 16 cm taller than the poppy.

Top Tip *Before trying to answer any questions about a graph, spend a little time studying and trying to understand it.*

I planted some cress last week but it hasn't grown at all yet.

It might help if you water it!

Have a go...

Grow some cress and check its height each day. Draw a bar chart to show the results.

Key words

bar chart   axis

scale

Quick Test

Use the graphs on these pages to answer these questions:

1. How many blackbirds were seen at the bird table?

2. How many more sparrows than robins were seen?

3. Which bird visited the bird table 10 times?

4. Which flower measured 22 cm tall?

5. Which flower is 15 cm shorter than the iris?

Test your skills

What is the weather like?

Use these different diagrams, charts and graphs to record the weather for a week... or longer!

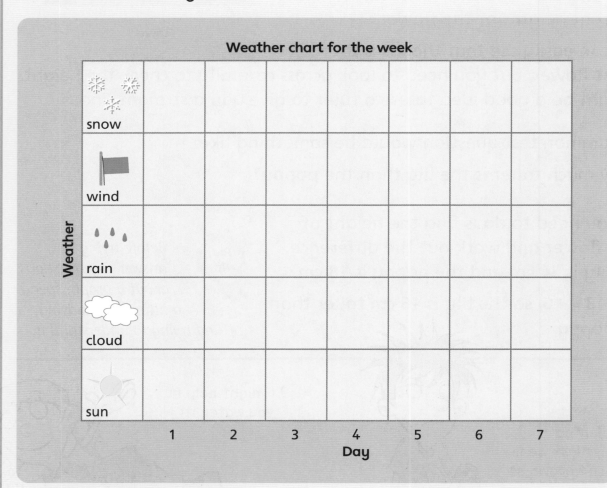

Weather chart for the week

Weather: snow, wind, rain, cloud, sun — Day 1 2 3 4 5 6 7

It's great when it's sunny and I can play outside!

Yes, it leaves me to read my book in peace!

Sunshine and temperature

Hours of sunshine

Saturday	
Sunday	
Monday	
Tuesday	
Wednesday	
Thursday	
Friday	

Key

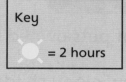 = 2 hours

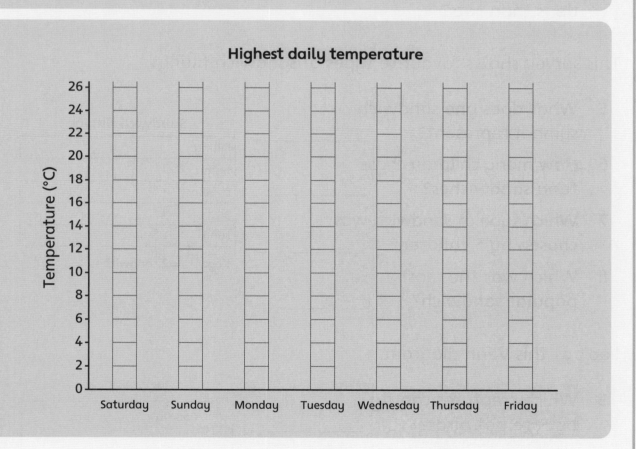

Look at the information you have collected. What have you found out about the weather?

Test your knowledge

Section 1

Types of pets owned by class 2B.

1 How many children have rabbits? _____

2 Which pet is the most popular? _____

3 How many children have birds? _____

4 How many more children have dogs than cats? _____

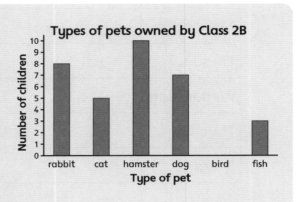

Types of pets owned by Class 2B

This survey shows favourite types of sandwich fillings.

5 What does one sandwich symbol represent? _____

6 How many children chose tuna sandwiches? _____

7 Which type of sandwich was chosen by 5 children? _____

8 Which was the most popular sandwich? _____

Sandwich fillings

Filling:				
ham	🍞	🍞	🍞	
cheese	🍞	🍞	🍞	🍞
egg	🍞			
tuna	🍞	🍞		

Key: 🍞 = 2 sandwiches

Look at this Venn diagram.

9 Which creatures can fly but are not birds? _____

_____

10 Which birds cannot fly? _____

_____

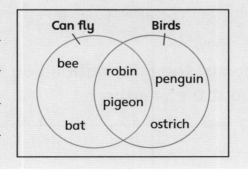

Section 2

Heights

1 Who is the shortest child?

_____

2 How tall is Sanjay?

_____

3 Which child is 98 cm tall?

_____

4 What is the difference in height between Hannah and Lucy?

_____

5 Which two children are the same height?

_____

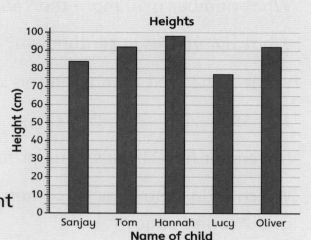

Skipping

6 Who skipped the greatest number of times?

_____

7 Who skipped 13 times?

_____

8 How many more times did Harry skip than David?

_____

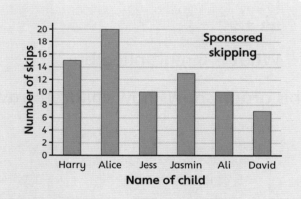

9 Who skipped the same number of times as Ali? _____

10 What was the total number of skips made by all the children together? _____

Test practice

1   What number is 10 more than 452?   _____

2   What is 4 metres in centimetres?   _____

3   What is the next number in this sequence?   _____

   17   19   _____   23   25   27

4   November has 31 days. True or false?   _____

5   Which solid shape has no corners, 3 faces and 2 round edges?   _____

6   Which of these angles is a right angle?   _____

   a    **b** 

7   44 + 45 = ?   _____

8   What is 6 multiplied by 3?   _____

This graph shows how children travel to school.

⟟ = 5 children	⟟ = 1 to 4 children			
car	⟟	⟟	⟟	⟟
bus	⟟	⟟		
walk	⟟	⟟		
cycle	⟟			

9   How many children travel by car?   _____

10 Do more children travel by bus or walk? _____

11 $27 \div 3 = ?$ _____

12 How many corners has a sphere got? _____

13 Tariq has £1 and he buys a pen for 45p and a rubber for 15p.

How much change will he have? _____

14 Is 20 a multiple of 4? _____

15 Write these numbers in order, starting with the smallest.

37　16　31　19　44　　　　　_____

16 How many sides has an octagon got? _____

17 Harry needs 18 cakes for his party and there are 4 cakes in a box. How many boxes of cakes will he need to make sure everyone gets one cake?

_____

18 Is 54 an odd or even number? _____

19 Estimate the position of each arrow.

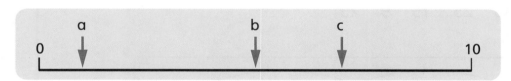

a _____　　b _____　　c _____

20 What time is shown on each of these clocks?

a _____　　b _____　　c _____

21 What number is 10 less than 98? _____

22 7 × 5 = ? _____

23 Which letter will the arrow point to if it moves a half turn clockwise? _____

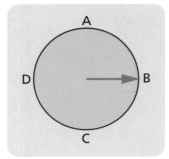

24 How many sides has a hexagon got? _____

25 Which number comes after seventeen? Is it 18 or 81? _____

26 What is 300 cm in metres? _____

27 A pair of shoes cost £35 but there is £9 off in a sale. What is the sale price? _____

28 33 + 34 = ? _____

29 Place these numbers correctly on this Venn diagram.

12   4   30   25   15   9   23

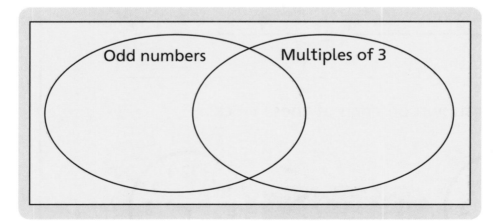

30 Which numbers are multiples of 3 and even? _____

31 Which day comes before Thursday? _____

32 What is the missing number?

30   35   ___   45   50 _____

33 53 − 9 = ? _____

34 Jasmin swims 20 m further than Ben.

Ben swims double the distance of Holly.

Holly swims 15 m.

How far did Jasmin swim? _____

35 How much juice is in this jug? _____

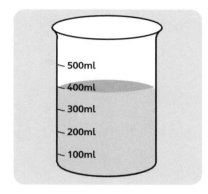

36 What is the largest number that can be made
from the digits 3, 7, and 5? _____

37 Is a teaspoon longer or shorter than 5 cm? _____

38 What position on the compass is
opposite west? _____

39 Name each of these shapes.

a _____   b _____   c _____

40 Which shape is not symmetrical – a, b, or c? _____

0	10	20	30	40
A bit more practice needed		Great try – check your errors	Fantastic – ready for the test!	

Answers

Numbers

PAGES 4–5 COUNTING PATTERNS

1 31, 32   2 23, 27   3 15, 25
4 70, 50   5 10, 8

PAGES 6–7 NUMBERS

1 15   2 145   3 273
4 477   5 764

PAGES 8–9 SPECIAL NUMBERS

1 odd   4 20
2 zero (and a tummy ache!)   5 110
3 yes

PAGES 10–11 COMPARING AND ORDERING

1 blue   2 54   3 10
4 19, 24, 27, 32, 38   5 98

PAGES 12–13 ESTIMATING

1 8   4 50
2 17   5 approximately 40
3 70

PAGES 14–15 FRACTIONS

1 $\frac{1}{4}$ 2 no   3 5
4 2   5 5

PAGES 18–19 TEST YOUR KNOWLEDGE

Section 1

1 40   7 84
2 76   8 12
3 62   9 there are:
4 115   a 6 flowers
5 8   b 8 caterpillars
6 an even number   c 7 bees

Section 2

1 a $\frac{1}{3}$ b $\frac{1}{2}$ c $\frac{1}{4}$ 5 40
2 72   6 yes
3 20   7 2
4 20

Section 3

1 12   4 a 4th
2 false   b lion
3 527   c clown

Calculations

PAGES 20–21 NUMBER FACTS

1 8   2 10   3 11
4 12   5 14   6 2
7 4   8 3   9 8
10 4

PAGES 22–23 ADDITION AND SUBTRACTION

1 110   2 25   3 18
4 41   5 15

PAGES 24–25 MULTIPLICATION AND DIVISION

1 16   2 yes   3 28
4 6   5 3

PAGES 26–27 TIMES TABLES

1 12   2 30   3 70
4 16   5 18   6 20
7 32   8 30   9 14
10 27

PAGES 28–29 PROBLEM-SOLVING

1 4   2 60p   3 90p
4 16p   5 20p

PAGES 32–33 TEST YOUR KNOWLEDGE

Section 1

1 7   2 1100   3 101
4 20   5 24   6 4
7 18   8 6   9 43p
10 a 90p
    b 54p
    c 95p

Section 2

1 25   2 41   3 35p
4 7   5 60   6 5
7 20   8 27

Section 3

1 a 30
    b 20
    c 10
2 16

Measures and shapes

PAGES 34–35 2-D SHAPES
1	hexagon	**2**	5	**3**	square
4	yes	**5**	quadrilateral	**6**	octagon

PAGES 36–37 3-D SOLIDS
1	cube	**2**	3	**3**	sphere
4	pyramid	**5**	cylinder; cone		

PAGES 38–39 POSITION AND TURNING
1	A2	**2**	east	**3**	C
4	B	**5**	north		

PAGES 40–41 MEASUREMENT
1	1000	**2**	true	**3**	20 g
4	mass	**5**	150		

PAGES 42–43 TIME
1	60	**2**	Thursday	**3**	September
4	9:20	**5**	9:35		

PAGES 46–47 TEST YOUR KNOWLEDGE

Section 1
1	pentagon	**6**	6	
2	60	**7**	9	
3	triangle	**8**	yes	
4	August	**9**	**a** 10.30 **b** 1.25 **c** 8.50	
5	square	**10**	c	

Section 2
1	north	**7**	east	
2	2 kg	**8**	starfish	
3	millilitres	**9**	crab	
4	5 cm	**10**	**a** flag	
5	false		**b** crab	
6	1000 ml		**c** bucket	

Handling data

PAGES 48–49 SORTING DIAGRAMS
1	Laura or Jordan	**3**	Ali or Jack	
2	David	**4**	Jo	

PAGES 50–51 PICTOGRAMS AND GRAPHS
1	2	**2**	green and red	**3**	15
4	1	**5**	3		

PAGES 52–53 GRAPHS AND CHARTS
1	5	**2**	6	**3**	blue tit
4	daisy	**5**	tulip		

PAGES 56–57 TEST YOUR KNOWLEDGE

Section 1
1	8	**2**	hamster	**3**	0
4	2	**5**	2 sandwiches	**6**	4
7	ham	**8**	cheese	**9**	bee and bat
10	penguin and ostrich				

Section 2
1	Lucy	**2**	84 cm	**3**	Hannah
4	20 cm	**5**	Tom and Oliver	**6**	Alice
7	Jasmin	**8**	8	**9**	Jess
10	75				

Test practice

1	462
2	400 cm
3	21
4	false
5	cylinder
6	b
7	89
8	18
9	20
10	by bus
11	9
12	none
13	40p
14	yes
15	16, 19, 31, 37, 44
16	8
17	5

18	an even number
19	**a** 1
	b 5
	c 7
20	**a** 6:45
	b 11:10
	c 2:30
21	88
22	35
23	D
24	6
25	18
26	3 metres
27	£26
28	67

29
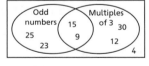

30	12 and 30
31	Wednesday
32	40
33	44
34	50 m
35	400 ml
36	753
37	longer
38	east
39	**a**: rectangle
	b: circle
	c: quadrilateral
40	c

Glossary

analogue clock shows the time using hands moving around a dial

approximate a 'rough' answer - near to the real answer

anti-clockwise turning in this direction

axis (plural is axes) the horizontal and vertical lines on a graph

bar chart a type of graph that has bars to show amounts

block graph a type of graph where each block means one amount

calculation Adding, taking away, multiplying and dividing are all calculations

capacity the amount of liquid a container holds

Carroll diagram a sorting diagram that shows groups of things in a grid

clockwise turning in this direction

corner where the edges or sides of shapes meet

difference the amount by which one number is greater than another. The difference between 9 and 14 is 5

digital clock shows the time using digits rather than by having hands on a dial

digits There are 10 digits: 0 1 2 3 4 5 6 7 8 and 9 that make all the numbers we use

divide to share or group; ÷ is the sign for divide

double To make something twice as big, or multiply by 2

dozen another word for twelve

edge where two faces of a solid shape meet

estimate is like a good guess

even numbers numbers that can be divided exactly by 2. They end in 0 2 4 6 or 8

face the flat side of a solid shape

fraction part of a whole one

half $\frac{1}{2}$ is one half, or one out of two parts

heptagon a shape with 7 straight sides

hexagon a shape with 6 straight sides

length how long an object is – could be measured in centimetres or metres

mass how much matter something contains; how heavy something is depends on its mass

multiply to count in groups, adding the same amount a certain number of times; × is the sign for multiply

multiples A multiple is a number made by multiplying together two other numbers

number bonds these are the addition and subtraction facts within 20

octagon a shape with 8 straight sides

odd numbers numbers that cannot be divided exactly by 2. Odd numbers always end in 1, 3, 5, 7 or 9

pentagon a shape with 5 straight sides

pictogram graphs that use symbols or pictures, where each symbol represents a certain number of items

quadrilateral a shape with 4 straight sides

right angle a quarter turn. The corner of a square is a right angle

rounding changing a number to the nearest ten. A 'round number' is a number ending in zero: 10, 20, 30, 40, 50, 60, 70, 80, 90 or 100

scale These are the labelled marks that show an amount on rulers, jugs and weighing scales

sequence a list of numbers which usually have a pattern. They are often numbers written in order

square a shape with four equal sides

symmetrical when two halves of a shape or pattern are identical

total when you add some numbers the answer is the total

tree diagram a way of sorting things into groups by asking questions

triangle a shape with 3 straight sides

Venn diagram a way of showing how different things can be sorted into groups, called sets

weight how heavy an object is

zero 0 or nothing